Buy to Let
on a Budget
How <u>You</u> Can Invest in Property with Minimal Finance!

Martin Woodward

ISBN: 978-1-4717-9460-5

Copyright © Martin Woodward - 2011
All rights reserved

Acknowledgments

To my brother Glyn Woodward of Woodward Associates Chartered Surveyors - Oxted Surrey for his kind help and assistance particularly regarding health and safety/fire regulations and condensation issues. Thanks Glyn!

Contents

ACKNOWLEDGMENTS 3
INTRODUCTION 7
BUYING 8
    When to Buy 8
    What to Buy 9
    Purpose Built Flat or Studio 9
    Flat in Converted House (or over shop) 10
    House for Multiple Occupancy 10
    Small House for Single/Couple Occupancy 11
    Family House 11
    Holiday Let - UK or Abroad 11
    Garage or Parking Space 14
    How to Buy 14
    Buying at Auctions 17
    Solicitors 17
YIELDS 19
    Net Profits 19
    Example 1 20
    Example 2 21
    Example 3 22
    Example 4 23
    Increasing Your Portfolio 24
PROPERTY VS COMMODITIES 26
TENANTS 33
    Unemployed DSS Claimants 33
    Students 34
    Professional Couples 35

    Single Professional People *35*
    Families with Children *35*
    Executive Lets *36*
    References *36*
    Tenants Rights *37*
    Contracts *38*
    Bonds and Advance Payments *39*
    Property Checks *40*
    Finding Tenants *41*
    The National Landlords Association *41*

FINANCING YOUR PROJECT 43
    Repayment Mortgages *43*
    Interest Only Mortgages *45*
    Endowment Mortgages *45*
    The Real Differences *46*
    Funding your First Deposit *47*

PRESENTATION 50
    Repairs and Renewals *53*
    EPC Energy Performance Certificates *54*
    Health and Safety *54*

AGENTS 56

COUNCIL TAX & UTILITIES 58
    Council Tax *58*
    Water Rates *58*
    Gas & Electricity *59*
    Telephone/Internet *60*
    T.V. Licence *60*
    Sky T.V. *60*
    Insurance *61*
    Community Fees & Ground Rents *61*

TAX 63

Income Tax *63*
Capital Gains Tax *64*
Other Books/Guides by Martin Woodward *69*

Introduction

Firstly, let me make it clear that the 'Buy to Let' property business is a very long term investment. And don't think that you need to be 'clever' to get into it - anyone can do it! I know what it's like to be unemployed with no qualifications and own absolutely nothing and I managed it, as have many immigrants who arrived in the UK penniless. You just need a bit of 'drive' and 'vision' - and of course the correct information, as found herein.

Saving for a pension the conventional way and then buying an annuity invariably incurs many hidden fees, but probably the worst thing is that you don't even have complete control of the situation, whereas with property this is not the case. If you start investing in property at age 45 - 50 or less, you should easily fund your pension far more effectively and far more affordably than any typical private pension scheme. And then you are free to buy an annuity as and when you wish, or not at all.

Many property investors are criticised as being 'fat cats' full of greed, which I think is grossly unfair as they provide a very valuable social service as any honest ethical business does. Sure they make a profit, but if they didn't, the essential service they offer would cease to exist.

But in order to be successful, you must get the balance right - follow the guidelines as herein, provide good, clean accommodation at a fair rent and you will be respected by both your tenants and your bank manager.

Forget wasting your money on designer clothes, expensive cars or overpriced meals, all of which are a complete waste of money. If you want financial independence, get into property and in a few years you can have all the other stuff without getting into debt.

Chapter 1

Buying

When to Buy

Needless to say, the best time to buy is near the bottom of a property crash. Judging exactly when this is is any ones guess, although after a big drop in prices you should be fairly safe. But even then you need to squeeze the price as low as possible.

Will prices ever rise again?

After every property boom and bust we are told that that's it for property prices - and we'll never see these sorts of rises again. Well I'm 63 years old (advancing steadily) and I've heard this said numerous times. Historically property prices double more or less every 7 or 8 years - this is fact! Check it out if you don't believe me. Sometimes the rise is constant and gradual and other times there are long 'flat' times of inactivity followed by sudden and substantial rises and then often a slight downward adjustment. But the underlying trend is always upward.

The truth is that we're constantly fed bull****! One moment we are told that property is at an all time high, then the next day or week we are told that there is an enormous shortage of housing (which is true) and that the population is exploding out of proportion and within the next 20 years or so we must have hundreds of thousands of new properties, just to stay as we are. And of course fuel and building costs are constantly going up in price and building land is becoming more and more scarce - so of course **property prices will continue to rise! This is a certainty!**

When asked 'how should one deal with negative equity?', even the worst pessimists who come out with all the negativity will say that if possible you should sit it out and wait for prices to rise again - even they know this is inevitable!

What to Buy

The best type of property to buy obviously depends on your finances and what type of tenants you hope to attract. Any property is rentable, but the size, location/convenience and quality will have a bearing on the price and how quickly the property will be let out. And of course it must be targeted to the right type of tenants.

Basically the choices are:

- Purpose built flat or studio;
- Flat in converted house (or over shop);
- House for multiple occupancy;
- Small house for single/couple occupancy;
- Family house;
- Holiday let - UK or Abroad;
- Garage or Parking Space.

Whatever you buy, look into any parking issues, and always buy with view to future selling, which one day will occur! And remember that in all cases (except land/garage) gas safety certificates will be required.

Purpose Built Flat or Studio

The big disadvantage of purpose built flats can be the management charges. Often these can be £1,000 per annum or more and this will generally be paid by the landlord - one more expense that you don't need! Also most flats tend to be leasehold, which can be a problem when you want to re-sell if there is less than 70 years left. But having said this, purpose built flats with a good management committee and reasonable charges do exist and can be a good bet.

Studios are quite rentable, but watch that you buy for a good price as they can be very difficult to resell. Some banks/building societies won't consider mortgaging them and these may also have expensive communal charges and ground rent.

The one property that I still let out is a stone built ground floor flat with its own entrance, garden and garage surrounded by parkland within only a 5 minute walk of Sheffield city centre - a superb investment property.

Flat in Converted House (or over shop)

Flats in converted houses or above shops, may or may not be leasehold and will probably not have communal charges. However, it needs to be clear exactly who is responsible for what. For instance, if your flat is downstairs, do you have a joint responsibility for repairing the roof and gutters? This is where a good management arrangement/committee is essential. With the above problems sorted, these can be ideal properties for investment.

House for Multiple Occupancy

If buying this type of property, your potential tenants would be either: students; single young professionals; or single unemployed, but probably not all together. The location of the property would determine which tenants it would be best for. But either way, this type of property could be the most profitable - see yields shortly.

If the property has 2/3 bedrooms and 2 reception rooms, the normal thing to do is to use one of the downstairs reception rooms as an additional bedroom and keep the other and the kitchen as communal areas.

An important point to bear in mind with this choice is that they are governed by strict 'fire regulations' which you must adhere to. These change regularly, so check before you buy. But basically, this could mean the compulsory installation of fire doors to all rooms and any rooms above the first floor will require a fire exit, so basically forget renting out attics.

Generally, with shared houses, the landlord pays the fuel bills, council tax and water rates, so these must be geared into the rent.

Another type of multiple occupancy property would be one that is split into self contained bed sits or flats. Then no communal areas (apart from the entrance hall) would be necessary and these could have their own utility meters. In most cases these would then be individually liable for council tax.

Personally, I've steered away from the multiple occupancy properties, but this has mainly been because I've always been too busy with other concerns. But there is no doubt that these *can* be the most profitable - but also the most hassle.

Small House for Single/Couple Occupancy

These are probably my favourite choice as they attract the tenants that I prefer. I've owned a few modern one bedroom properties which have the advantage over flats that they are usually freehold; don't have communal charges and often have their own off road parking.

I've also owned two bedroom Victorian terraced properties which can be good, but can also be money pits if you get it wrong (from the maintenance point of view).

Family House

This could be anything from a 3 bed ex council house upwards and of course is ideal if you want to attract family tenants either DSS or professionals. These properties would most likely be suitable as unfurnished lettings and in this case the tenants would probably stay for a longer term. These can be an excellent proposition if bought for the right price.

Holiday Let - UK or Abroad

Holiday lets come into a different category from all the others and most landlords would choose to deal in only one or the other but rarely both, although I have.

If you happen to live in a holiday location then these can be a superb proposition, but the majority are seasonal, meaning you would achieve high rents (usually weekly) during the season and little or nothing off season.

The other downside is that they're much more labour intensive, as you would have to arrange laundry and cleaning virtually every weekend in the summer months. Plus of course there would be much more administration and advertising involved.

Forget caravans unless you own the caravan site or unless you live in a holiday destination and have one in your garden - then you could be on to a winner. But on a caravan site, the site fees, initial purchase cost and depreciation make these totally unviable from a business point of view - the only winners in this situation are the site owners.

One of the best propositions shown in one of the recent TV house buying programmes was a terraced property in Ross on Wye with a self contained one bedroom chalet at the end of the garden - a home with an income! - Superb!

Properties abroad can be fraught with dangers. They are rarely what they seem and always involve hidden buying and selling fees. This generally makes them unprofitable and bad investments or in some cases a complete disaster.

I've personally owned properties in France, Spain and Cyprus. I did make profits in Cyprus, but it has to be said that I would have made much more had the same funds been invested in the UK property market during the same period.

The problems with letting foreign properties are:

- a) If you live in the UK, you will probably find clients fairly easily, but are likely to have problems with cleaning and maintenance;
- b) If you live where the properties are, you will be able to deal with the cleaning and maintenance issues yourself easily, but are likely to have problems finding clients as they are reluctant to phone non UK telephone numbers;

c) Either way, you will still be liable for income tax either where the properties are or in the UK (but not both) and some countries charge an annual tax based on the property value regardless of whether you rent them out or not.

I've done this both living in the UK and in Cyprus and I can tell you that by and large it's a lot of grief for a low reward.

These 'buy a house in the sun' T.V. programmes make me laugh when they say how much rent a holiday property will supposedly return - it's possible to make anything look good 'hypothetically'!

If buying abroad consider the following:

a) Don't buy without titles deeds. This rules out many off plan new properties;

b) Make sure that titles deeds are what you think they are. This rules out Northern Cyprus as the deeds are issued illegally;

c) Never borrow money that is reliant on rental income;

d) Think very carefully before taking out a non sterling mortgage;

e) Check for debts tied to the property. In Spain if you buy a property, you also buy all the debts that are attached to it, and these could be far more than the value of the property;

f) Make sure that the property has the full legal building permission both locally *and* nationally;

g) Have the property surveyed. I've seen numerous foreign properties literally falling down through incompetent builders;

h) Have a legal Will drawn up in the country in question;

i) Double check all buying AND selling fees. In Spain you can typically add about 14% on top for buying fees, but what no one will tell you is that there will be a retention on selling in lieu of capital gains tax which theoretically you can claim back but in practice costs more than it's worth in legal fees;

j) Make sure that the price you pay is the price that is declared in the contract and entered on the deeds. It's common practice to under declare to avoid property tax, but they simply get this back through capital gains tax when you sell;

k) In most countries local solicitors will simply deal with the purchase, but won't necessarily advise you if you are buying a 'lemon' or that the seller actually owns the property. And very often they will have the seller's interest in mind and not yours. Use a UK solicitor who specialises in foreign property sales;

l) Remember that in some countries you can be imprisoned for debt.

If you need to know more about Cyprus see my guide 'Living and Working in Cyprus - the Good, the Bad and the Ugly'. Much of the information in this guide also applies to other foreign destinations.

Garage or Parking Space

Don't laugh at this option. If you cannot get finance to buy anything more, town centre parking spaces or garages usually return the highest yields and can be a low cost step into the property game!

Similarly even a paddock or woodland could also offer a worthwhile yield - check it out!

How to Buy

Before we discuss *how to buy*, we'll briefly look at how *not* to buy.

With any worthwhile venture, there will always be sharks out there waiting to rip you off. Just before the last property price crash, such sharks were there selling seminars for £2,000+ where they promised to give the latest inside information and sell ideal properties 'at rock bottom prices' that were 'guaranteed' to increase in value . Most of these properties turned out to be purpose built city centre apartments that were often badly built, hugely over priced and had grossly over inflated management charges.

No doubt these companies produced glossy brochures with attractive looking but totally unrealistic profit projections. As I'm sure you are aware, after the crash, many of those taken in by these scams went bankrupt, losing not only their investments, but also the homes that they lived in. Then the clever investors stepped in and bought up these properties for less than half of the original price!

My advice to you would be, stay away from seminars, buy in an area that *you* know, and trust your own judgement! You would be mad to buy in a town that you knew nothing about. *You know* the desirable/undesirable areas in your locality and where the students and young professionals hang out! *You know* the areas where you'd be lucky to make it to the end of the road if walking after dark! But don't think that you have to buy in the best areas, just not the worst!

But most importantly, only buy what you can comfortably afford. No doubt at some time you've played Monopoly where everyone starts off with the same £1,500, yet all the property prices vary. Have you noticed that winning Monopoly, in most cases is achieved by buying the low to mid priced properties and plastering them with hotels? Buying the high priced ones first will just get rid of all your cash leaving you with nothing to expand with. Doing it for real is actually easier as you're not so reliant on the 'luck' of the dice and you've less chance of ending up in jail - but don't rule this out!

I've found that for the best deals you need to find either empty properties (perhaps where someone has died) or properties where the sellers are desperate to get out (for whatever reason).

Check price web sites (such as http://www.zoopla.com) to see what similar properties have sold for recently in the same vicinity and obviously take into account the condition of the property and how much it would cost you to bring it up to spec. And check potential rents and yield (which we'll deal with shortly).

Of course you should make all the obvious checks for damp; subsidence; wood rot; dodgy electrics and roofs etc. You will be forced to pay for a basic valuation if you are borrowing from a bank or building society and although this may highlight anything really negative, you are recommended to have the next level of inspection, such as the Homebuyers Report. Although this may cost a bit more, it's also better to have this done independently of the mortgage valuation (if applicable). In some cases a full structural survey is advisable and in many cases the cost of these can be reclaimed by re-negotiating the purchase price as a result of the surveyor's findings.

Having found a suitable property, arrange a mortgage 'in principle' with your bank or building society, making it clear to them that you are 'buying to let'. Then make your first bid ridiculously low. Don't worry about being laughed at or insulted. And don't feel intimidated by the seller's agents. Every property that I've ever bought has been under priced and the way I see it, it has just given me a fighting chance. Remember you can always increase your bid if you really want to, but you can rarely lower it again. And if you don't get the deal you want - walk away - there will be more!

One of my better deals was for a modern one bed townhouse where the owner had been taken into a nursing home. The relatives, who showed me round, told me that all the proceeds of the sale would be taken by the social security to fund the nursing home, so they said from their point of view they didn't care what it sold for. The asking price at the time was £28,500. I offered £15,000 and the agents laughed at me, then the offer was accepted (I wish I'd offered less). Not expecting to be successful, I had no financing in place, so I put it on a credit card for a couple of years bouncing it between cards to get 0% interest, then (as I didn't particularly want it anyway), I sold it on complete with tenant for £30,000. And as it was in joint names with my wife, we also avoided all the capital gains tax - more about this later.

Buying at Auctions

The first thing that you need to be aware of when buying at auctions is that you will have effectively exchanged contracts at the fall of the hammer and consequently will be committed to complete the purchase. Fail to complete and you will lose your 10% deposit and possibly also get sued for further costs. So you must get your finances in order *before* you bid. If you need a mortgage or loan this will probably mean paying for a survey on the property even though your bid may be unsuccessful. And if arranging a mortgage in principal with your bank, make sure that you have something binding in writing before bidding. I've twice been promised a 'mortgage in principal' only to be let down at the last moment, fortunately, not when I'd been bidding at an auction. This is the sort of reliability that you can expect from the banks - I've learnt not to trust any of them!

I'm sure that there are good deals to be acquired at auctions, but I would be inclined to leave it until you have at least six properties and are able to buy cash, or at least by releasing equity.

Solicitors

In order to buy safely, you will need the services of a solicitor or conveyancer. I've often thought about doing all this myself, but there are so many potential pitfalls, it's simply not worth it.

As with all professionals, their fees vary considerably, for basically the exact same service, so shop around. I've used expensive ones and cheaper ones and to be honest there's not a lot to choose.

My personal experience of solicitors has not been good. Out of the ones I've used:

- One ended up imprisoned for multiple murder (he's probably out now so watch out for him);
- Two were imprisoned for embezzlement;

- One absconded to South Africa with over £1 million of clients funds;
- Two lost my title deeds (incredible but true); and
- One totally messed up the property searches, and then denied all knowledge of it.

Maybe I've just been unlucky, but for me the joke: '99% of solicitors give the rest a bad name' - is true!

I did actually find a very good one called Mike Haslam, but unfortunately I don't know where he is now.

Chapter 2

Yields

The yield is the single most important factor to consider when buying a property - ignore this at your peril. The yield (or rather *potential* yield), is the percentage of rent received in relation to the purchase price of the property. For instance if the purchase price is £100k and the annual rent is £5k, then the yield is 5% - although you would rarely achieve this!

When considering buying, I would always be inclined to include any essential refurbishment costs on top of the purchase price, before calculating the potential yield. And always be realistic when considering the potential rent - look at what similar properties in the same area let out for and never be over optimistic.

When interest rates are low a 5% yield may seem attractive, but remember that yield is **not** profit, nor is it guaranteed. Very often cheaper properties with low rents have much higher potential yields than better, more expensive properties and therefore can often be far better investments. On the surface it doesn't seem to make sense.

Net Profits

In the first few years it's doubtful that you'd get anywhere near making a net profit even if your property is fully let for every month in the year. So you may ask - why do it? The answer to this is, for long term *capital* appreciation which is not shown in the annual profit/loss accounts, but is the main factor that most investors are in the business. And of course while ever you don't make a net profit, you won't pay any income tax.

We'll now look at a few hypothetical examples and see how they pan out.

Example 1

Assuming a property costs £100,000 and achieves an annual rent of £4,800 (4.8% yield), was purchased with a 75% mortgage at 6% interest and is let out for the full 12 months. The annual summary of accounts would look something like the following chart:

Total Income (12 months)	£4,800.00
Less 10% Wear & Tear	£480.00
Total Income (12 months)	£4,320.00
Agents Fees 10%	£480.00
Mortgage Interest	£4,500.00
Gas Certificate	£100.00
Repairs/renewals	£200.00
Buildings Insurance	£300.00
Expenses	£5,580.00
Net Profit/Loss	**-£1,260.00**

In all the examples I have assumed full 12 month occupancy but you must be prepared for unoccupied periods which most certainly *will* occur. I've also included a few obvious estimated expenses, but again you must be prepared for more.

It can be seen from these figures that a loss has occurred even though the maximum rent has been achieved. However a saving could be made by not using an agent and the 10% wear and tear allowance is simply a tax allowance that you would not have actually paid out. Taking these into account the loss would have been less.

But, before you get too excited, none of the examples include the *capital* payments on the mortgages which are not a tax deductible expense and therefore not included in the tax accounts summary. This amount would be nil if you have an interest only mortgage (not recommended), or initially £2,038 per annum gradually increasing as the interest reduces which will be explained later.

So it should be clear that a 5% yield is far from self financing and could be far worse if you didn't receive the income as predicted (for whatever reason), or had any unexpected repairs.

But don't despair, as there are real profits in the form of capital growth in a few years - remember it's not a short term investment! In 7 - 8 years this property will probably be worth £200,000, giving you a 100% capital gain and the rent will also have potentially increased, but your mortgage repayments will be the same (apart from any mortgage interest rate fluctuations up or down)!

Now we'll look at another example with a lower purchase cost but a higher yield.

Example 2

Assuming a property costs £50,000 and achieves an annual rent of £4,200 (8.4% yield), was purchased with a 75% mortgage at 6% interest and is let for the full 12 months. The annual summary of accounts would look something like the following chart:

Total Income (12 months)	£4,200.00
Less 10% Wear & Tear	£420.00
Total Income (12 months)	£3,780.00
Agents Fees 10%	£420.00
Mortgage Interest	£2,250.00
Gas Certificate	£100.00
Repairs/renewals	£200.00
Buildings Insurance	£300.00
Expenses	£3,270.00
Net Profit/Loss	**£510.00**

In this example the annual capital repayments would initially be £1,019 per annum making this property much easier to cope with should things not go according to plan, but of course the capital gain would be only half of the last example.

Now we'll look at an example of a multiple occupancy property.

Example 3

Assuming a property costs £80,000 and achieves an annual rent of £12,000 (15% yield), was purchased with a 75% mortgage at 6% interest and is let out for 12 months with full occupancy. The annual summary of accounts would look something like the following chart:

Total Income (12 months)	£12,000.00
Less 10% Wear & Tear	£1,200.00
Total Income (12 months)	£10,800.00
Agents Fees 10%	£1,200.00
Mortgage Interest	£3,600.00
Gas Certificate	£100.00
Utility Costs	£2,000.00
Council Tax	£1,200.00
Repairs/renewals	£200.00
Buildings Insurance	£300.00
Expenses	£8,600.00
Net Profit/Loss	**£2,200.00**

This is based on a three bed property with 2 downstairs rooms, one of which is used as an additional bedroom, keeping a communal lounge, kitchen and bathroom.

In this example the capital repayments will initially be £1,631 per annum and would also have a good potential capital gain.

Notice here that you will also normally have to pay the council tax and fuel costs (unless you can figure out a way of doing it differently), and this of course is the reason that tenants will pay £250 per month for a room as these other costs are normally inclusive in the rent.

Obviously, the last example appears to be the most attractive, especially when you deduct the £1,200 wear and tear allowance and possibly the agent's fees.

But this doesn't mean that I particularly advise the multiple occupancy route. Although potentially very profitable, it can also be fraught with many problems, especially if dealing with DSS tenants or students, who would be the main clients for this type of tenancy. Plus you would also have to deal with additional fire regulations.

Having said this, if you get it right it can work very well. I actually lived in one of these houses many years ago and the guy who owned it also lived there. Everyone was friends with one another, making it a great place to live and the owner ended up getting his property basically for free courtesy of the tenants who were all very happy to live there.

Example 4

Typically the rent you'd get per month for a normal let you'd get per week for a holiday let, but not all year and as mentioned earlier you'd have to arrange cleaning/laundry etc. or do it yourself. And remember that the utilities and council tax (or business rates) would be payable by you, so all of these would need gearing into the rent. Consequently the chart shown maybe a long way from the actual figures, but will give you a rough guide only.

Assuming a holiday property costs £100,000 and achieves an annual rent of £8,400 (8.4% yield), based on 7 months occupancy at an average of £1,200, was purchased with a 75% mortgage at 6% interest.

In this example the capital repayments will initially be £2,038 per annum and the property would also have a good potential capital gain.

Total Income (7 months)	£8,400.00
Less 10% Wear & Tear	£840.00
Adjusted Income	£7,560.00
Advertising 10%	£840.00
Cleaning/maintenance	£1,000.00
Utilities	£1,000.00
Mortgage Interest	£4,500.00
Business Rates	£1,200.00
Insurance	£300.00
Gas Certificate	£100.00
Repairs/renewals	£200.00
Expenses	£9,140.00
Net Profit Loss	**-£1,580.00**

Do remember that in all cases as time passes and the value of your properties increases, affectively so does your yield. For instance the property that I have retained was originally purchased in 1997 for £28k and is now worth approx £110k and returns a rent of £550 which equates to 5% at today's valuation but 20% on the original price!

Increasing Your Portfolio

Once you've established your first letting property, it's surprisingly easy (possibly too easy) to expand. And the more you expand the easier it becomes. As soon as your first property has appreciated in value by 20 - 30% (in maybe 2 - 3 years), the equity could be used as a deposit for your next property and the projected yield could be included in your income computations. Then in another 2 - 3 years you should have even more equity from your first property, plus also some from your second, possibly enabling you to buy two more etc., etc.

BUT, don't get too greedy and always be prepared for non payments of rent for whatever reason, unexpected repairs and the next property crash. When you have *unused* equity in at least half of your portfolio, you will be in a fairly safe position and should easily be able to cope with any problems.

Eventually, your main problem will be how to minimise your capital gains tax liability when you decide to 'cash in' your investments, and then it all becomes worthwhile. But even this should be planned by taking the correct actions right at the beginning, which could save you literally thousands. Full details of this will be dealt with in a later chapter.

Chapter 3

Property vs Commodities

You may or may not know how commodity trading works, so I'll explain it as briefly and simply as possible.

A commodity could be any*thing,* for example: orange juice, wheat, barley, gold, silver oil etc. Most of these are listed in the Financial Times commodity trading pages.

Obviously at some point these commodities are actually bought by bakers to make bread, jewellers to make jewellery and oil companies to make petrol etc. But along the way they are traded back and forth by numerous speculators.

You may have heard of the term *'futures'* in relation to commodities. This is when a commodity is *'sold'* for a future delivery date at a price determined and fixed in the present.

What the heck has this got to do with property?

A lot! - Please just stay with me and you'll see the very important comparisons.

For our example we're going to use gold. We'll assume that you have done a great deal of research and you are absolutely 100% convinced that gold is grossly undervalued and will rally in price at some point during the coming year.

We'll assume that gold is trading at £950 per troy ounce (I know it's not but let's just assume that it is, to keep the figures fairly simple) and a gold contract on the commodity market consists of 100 ounces (£95,000).

Now if you had £95,000 you could simply buy the contract for immediate delivery, sit on your gold bars and wait for them to increase in value. Job done!

But if you didn't have £95,000 you could buy the *right to buy* and/or trade a gold contract for future delivery, say in 12 months, but at *today's* price. As there is a time element in the deal, the cost is increased to take interest into account, so the gold price in this event will be £1,000 per troy ounce (£100,000 for the contract).

In order to enter this arrangement you would have to pay a deposit, which is called a margin and this is likely to be about 5% - £5,000.

Now it's important to understand that this will give you the *right to buy* or trade the gold contract at today's price at any time during the life of the agreement. But just as importantly you will also be *obligated to buy* it at the agreed price at the end of the agreement unless you settle and close the position beforehand.

And having entered into this agreement, you would benefit from any future price rises and suffer any price reductions.

Ok, so having entered this agreement, let's assume that after say one month the price of the gold (futures) increases to £1,050 per troy ounce. Your position would then be *in profit* to the tune of £5,000 as shown in the chart below.

	Margin	1st Price	2nd Price	Positions	Exposure	Profit
	£ 5,000	£ 1,000	£ 1,050	1	£ 100,000	£ 5,000
Tls	£ 5,000			1	£ 100,000	£ 5,000

First Position

Now you could then close the position and take your £5,000 profit along with the return of your margin which computes to a 100% profit in one month, even though gold prices have only increased by 5% - not bad eh?

But having seen the potential of all this, you're far too greedy to leave it at that and anyway you are convinced that gold is going to skyrocket, not just go up a measly 5%. So instead of closing the position and taking your profit, you leave the position open and use the profit (which you'd be allowed to use) as the margin for an additional position (this time starting at £1,050 per troy ounce).

Now assuming during the next month that gold prices continued rising as you anticipate and reach £1,100 per troy ounce. Your positions would show another £5,000 profit on the first position and a further £5,000 profit on your second position as shown below.

	Second Position					
	Margins	1st Price	2nd Price	Positions	Exposure	Profit
	£ 5,000	£ 1,000	£ 1,100	1	£ 100,000	£ 10,000
	£ 5,250	£ 1,050	£ 1,100	1	£ 105,000	£ 5,000
Tls	£ 10,250			2	£ 205,000	£ 15,000

Again, you could close your positions and take your profit. But you're far too greedy for that, and anyway you are still convinced that gold prices will increase far more. So you use your profits to buy a further two contracts.

And as you anticipated, prices rose again to £1,150 and then £1,200 as you carried on doubling up your positions as shown below.

	Third Position					
	Margins	1st Price	2nd Price	Positions	Exposure	Profit
	£ 5,000	£ 1,000	£ 1,150	1	£ 100,000	£ 15,000
	£ 5,250	£ 1,050	£ 1,150	1	£ 105,000	£ 10,000
	£ 11,000	£ 1,100	£ 1,150	2	£ 220,000	£ 10,000
Tls	£ 21,250			4	£ 425,000	£ 35,000

	Fourth Position					
	Margins	1st Price	2nd Price	Positions	Exposure	Profit
	£ 5,000	£ 1,000	£ 1,200	1	£ 100,000	£ 20,000
	£ 5,250	£ 1,050	£ 1,200	1	£ 105,000	£ 15,000
	£ 11,000	£ 1,100	£ 1,200	2	£ 220,000	£ 20,000
	£ 23,000	£ 1,150	£ 1,200	4	£ 460,000	£ 20,000
Tls	£ 44,250			8	£ 885,000	£ 75,000

Now you will see that you could close these positions and take profits at £75,000, which you have to admit is an amazing return for your original £5,000 margin. But note also that at this point your exposure in the market is £885,000.

But you're on a roll and still convinced that gold prices are well on the up, which they are, so you carry on as shown in the next few charts.

Fifth Position

Margins	1st Price	2nd Price	Positions	Exposure	Profit
£ 5,000	£ 1,000	£ 1,250	1	£ 100,000	£ 25,000
£ 5,250	£ 1,050	£ 1,250	1	£ 105,000	£ 20,000
£ 11,000	£ 1,100	£ 1,250	2	£ 220,000	£ 30,000
£ 23,000	£ 1,150	£ 1,250	4	£ 460,000	£ 40,000
£ 48,000	£ 1,200	£ 1,250	8	£ 960,000	£ 40,000
Tls £ 92,250			16	£ 1,845,000	£ 155,000

Sixth Position

Margins	1st Price	2nd Price	Positions	Exposure	Profit
£ 5,000	£ 1,000	£ 1,300	1	£ 100,000	£ 30,000
£ 5,250	£ 1,050	£ 1,300	1	£ 105,000	£ 25,000
£ 11,000	£ 1,100	£ 1,300	2	£ 220,000	£ 40,000
£ 23,000	£ 1,150	£ 1,300	4	£ 460,000	£ 60,000
£ 48,000	£ 1,200	£ 1,300	8	£ 960,000	£ 80,000
£ 100,000	£ 1,250	£ 1,300	16	£ 2,000,000	£ 80,000
Tls £ 192,250			32	£ 3,845,000	£ 315,000

Seventh Position

Margins	1st Price	2nd Price	Positions	Exposure	Profit
£ 5,000	£ 1,000	£ 1,350	1	£ 100,000	£ 35,000
£ 5,250	£ 1,050	£ 1,350	1	£ 105,000	£ 30,000
£ 11,000	£ 1,100	£ 1,350	2	£ 220,000	£ 50,000
£ 23,000	£ 1,150	£ 1,350	4	£ 460,000	£ 80,000
£ 48,000	£ 1,200	£ 1,350	8	£ 960,000	£ 120,000
£ 100,000	£ 1,250	£ 1,350	16	£ 2,000,000	£ 160,000
£ 208,000	£ 1,300	£ 1,350	32	£ 4,160,000	£ 160,000
Tls £ 400,250			64	£ 8,005,000	£ 635,000

Now you will see that you could close these positions and take profits at £635,000, but if gold prices really did rally as you anticipate and rose to £2,000 per troy ounce the profits would be £4,795,000 as shown below - phenomenal!

Seventh Position (Alternative 1)

	Margins	1st Price	2nd Price	Positions	Exposure	Profit
	£ 5,000	£ 1,000	£ 2,000	1	£ 100,000	£ 100,000
	£ 5,250	£ 1,050	£ 2,000	1	£ 105,000	£ 95,000
	£ 11,000	£ 1,100	£ 2,000	2	£ 220,000	£ 180,000
	£ 23,000	£ 1,150	£ 2,000	4	£ 460,000	£ 340,000
	£ 48,000	£ 1,200	£ 2,000	8	£ 960,000	£ 640,000
	£ 100,000	£ 1,250	£ 2,000	16	£ 2,000,000	£ 1,200,000
	£ 208,000	£ 1,300	£ 2,000	32	£ 4,160,000	£ 2,240,000
Tls	£ 400,250			64	£ 8,005,000	£ 4,795,000

But, unbeknown to you Richard Branson with his team of experts is up on the moon in his space rocket. He's gone to the far side of the moon where no one else has been before and low and behold he discovers that it's not made of cheese as previously thought - it's made of gold! That's why it's got that sort of golden shimmery look to it! Any fool could have figured it out!

Now not only has he found the stuff, he also announces that he can bring it all down to Earth very economically. So what happens now? Gold prices take an unprecedented overnight dive to £500 per troy ounce and this happens so quickly that no one has time to close their contracts.

So what happens to you? You've shit it BIG TIME as shown in the next chart - **minus £4,805,000.**

Seventh Position (Alternative 2)

	Margins	1st Price	2nd Price	Positions	Exposure	Profit
	£ 5,000	£ 1,000	£ 500	1	£ 100,000	-£ 50,000
	£ 5,250	£ 1,050	£ 500	1	£ 105,000	-£ 55,000
	£ 11,000	£ 1,100	£ 500	2	£ 220,000	-£ 120,000
	£ 23,000	£ 1,150	£ 500	4	£ 460,000	-£ 260,000
	£ 48,000	£ 1,200	£ 500	8	£ 960,000	-£ 560,000
	£ 100,000	£ 1,250	£ 500	16	£ 2,000,000	-£ 1,200,000
	£ 208,000	£ 1,300	£ 500	32	£ 4,160,000	-£ 2,560,000
Tls	£ 400,250			64	£ 8,005,000	-£ 4,805,000

You don't even have enough noughts on your calculator to work out how much you're in debt! Never mind: 'Show me the way to Amarillo', it's: 'Show me the way to Beachy Head' (or Flamborough Head if you live up North)! I suppose you could max out your credit card one last time and get off to Paris and jump off a bridge there - but you'd be 'in Seine' if you did so!

This is God's way of kicking you in the nuts for being greedy!

You may be familiar with the Gospel according to St. Marmaduke, chapter 15 verse 12: *"And thy greed will be rewarded by a kick in the bollocks!"*

It's frightening to realise how quickly profits *and losses* can be generated in this business. In fact all of the above could have happened in a single day. And this is basically how 'rogue traders' lose all their money (or rather somebody else's money).

You could have incidentally, protected the positions by buying *'long put options'* and saved yourself the inconvenience of suicide. But this is another story altogether and of course these come at a premium.

Ok, but what the heck has this got to do with property?

Well, it may not be listed in the Financial Times commodity section, but property *is* a commodity, although fortunately not as *volatile* as most. And if you buy it with a mortgage you are buying a *'future'*.

You must realise that if you buy property on a mortgage, **it doesn't belong to you** - it belongs to the bank or building society! Your position would be exactly the same as shown above. All you are buying is 'control' of the property and the right AND OBLIGATION to buy it at the sale price at a later date (the end of the mortgage).

Sure if you have a repayment mortgage, you will be making payments off the capital throughout, but if you have an interest only mortgage as many investors go for (which I don't recommend incidentally) the position is exactly the same as a *'future'*.

And if you use all your equity, to increase your portfolio then you will be doing exactly the same as the examples shown and would be exposed to a similar risk (dependant on how many properties you buy).

Don't get me wrong, I'm not suggesting that you shouldn't do it - far from it. I'm just warning you of the risks in the unlikely event that you over expose yourself at the wrong time.

But as I said earlier, property *will* continue to increase in value, but as with all *commodities,* there will be upturns, downturns and times of non activity.

Never forget the Gospel according to St. Marmaduke chapter 15 verse 12! And make sure that you always keep Beachy Head programmed into your 'satnav'- just in case!

And if you make a disastrous mistake in some foreign countries, you won't have to worry about how to commit suicide; they'll take care of it for you!

Chapter 4

Tenants

Obviously the tenants are the life blood of the whole business, so you must be aware of the different types of tenants and market your properties accordingly.

Tenants fall into the following categories:

- Unemployed;
- Students;
- Professional couples;
- Single professionals;
- Families with children;
- Executive lets.

We'll look at these in more detail.

Unemployed DSS Claimants

When I first started work in the mid 60's I was shocked to see adverts for housing in the London Evening Standard and Evening News which regularly stated 'no blacks' and even used words that I dare not repeat. Although clearly racist and clearly wrong, at the time this was considered quite normal.

Obviously, now to even speak in such a way would be an illegal act, but apparently it's still ok and apparently quite normal to openly put 'no DSS' in housing adverts. Unfortunately, these poor souls have few rights. This is clear discrimination, but unfortunately these individuals have no-one to speak up for them.

Having said all this, renting out to anyone on benefits can be a problem as the rent will be set by the housing department (who will pay the rent) and *they* will decide what a fair rent is. In many cases, if you have bought properties with DSS in mind (perhaps ex council houses/flats or shared houses), this can be ok and can work very well.

However, in the past (if arranged) the housing department would pay the rent direct to the landlord and everything worked reasonably well. But recently, the powers that be have decided that the rent should be paid to the tenant and then *they* should pay the landlord. In the case of good honest individuals, this also works, but unfortunately not everyone is good and honest. And of course once a tenant is in one of your properties, getting them out is one heck of a problem, even if they decide not to pay the rent - more about this later. This situation is currently under review and will probably revert back to the previous system which worked well.

A good alternative, if you have the right type of properties for this type of tenant is to let the properties direct to a housing association for a pre-determined period. In this event, you would be guaranteed a specific payment from the housing association and they would have the problem of collecting rent and also sort out any damages etc., at the end of the tenancy. Obviously following this route would be less profitable, but for certain properties could be an excellent way.

Students

As shown in the yield examples, the shared properties are going to give you the best returns by far and these are the properties that will mainly appeal to students.

If this is your intention, you would need to make sure that the properties are in the right area and convenient for the college's etc., but I'm probably stating the obvious here!

Although offering possibly the highest returns, students will also give you the highest degree of grief. If you've ever seen the old T.V. series 'The Young Ones', about a shared house full of idiots, this more or less says it all!

In a shared house that I lived in a very long time ago, every time anyone needed a cup, they had to dig deep into a sink full of grease. The fridge got into such a bad state of needing defrosting that the ice forced the door off its hinges. No-one had any idea if there was a vacuum cleaner and probably wouldn't have known how to work it if they found one! And we used to pride ourselves in the fact that we caught all the mice *live*, and evicted them a few streets away - but they probably came straight back! Having said all this, it was a great place to live at the time!

Professional Couples

A professional (or rather working) couple has always been my first choice of tenant as they are generally reasonably reliable and usually pay the rent.

To attract this type of tenant, you would need either a one/two bedroom flat or house in a convenient location. Off road car parking would naturally be an advantage, but not always essential.

I always make a stipulation in the contract disallowing pets, as if they are working there would be no-one around to look after them. A couple of times this has been ignored and to be honest there's not a lot you can do about it. In this event, I've just informed them that it is a breach of the tenancy, and they will be charged for any damage caused. The same problem occurs with smoking.

Single Professional People

As with professional couples, the single professionals are generally fine and would be attracted by the same properties as the couples. Looking back, I think that this category has given me less problems than any other.

As well as a small one/two bed property, this category may also be ideal for a shared property.

Families with Children

Within this category would be two significant types; professional (working) and unemployed on benefits.

From a landlord's point of view, both could be good and profitable but would require different types of properties. In both cases, probably unfurnished would be more suitable, and in this event, they would probably also stay for a longer term.

Depending on exactly which type you are targeting, anything between a two bedroom ex-council house up to a four/five bedroom luxury detached property would be ideal. But in all cases - check yields and remember that a £500k property won't necessarily bring in ten times more rent than a £50k property. In fact you'd be lucky if it brings in five times!

Executive Lets

The executive let as the name suggests would be a very up market property (either house or apartment) in a convenient location of an up market area. This is the only type of property where top quality fittings are necessary, but of course this should also be reflected in the rent.

I would not recommend that a novice investor should attempt this type of let as the rewards *per cost involved* are no better than letting ex council houses to DSS claimants but the risk is far greater as these tenants are just as likely to default on the rent. Don't be fooled by their flashy cars and posh talk, they may be nearly bankrupt or as my wife says: 'All fur coat and no knickers!'

References

In all cases you must obtain written references from prospective tenants former landlords, employers and banks. If using an agent, they should do this for you. But if you do it yourself, it's a very good move to arrange to see the tenant at their current property. This will give you a chance to see how they live and find out why they want to leave etc. If a tenant is unable to provide suitable references, do not consider them. You would also be wise to write to referees yourself, rather than accepting references from the tenants as these could be forged - as I've personally experienced on a few occasions.

When a previous tenant of yours moves on to another property or decides to buy, they may well ask you for a reference, which of course you should provide. However make it quite clear to them that you will not give references if they default on their rent without very good reason or if they withhold the last month's rent in lieu of the bond.

Tenants Rights

As well as all the 'tenants rights' that are listed in the Short hold tenants contract, when it comes down to any potential court actions, you can be sure that although there are rights for landlords, the rights are heavily weighted on the side of the tenants - and they know it!

If a tenant breaches the contract, the landlord has the right to remove the tenant - but not without grief. This basically means that having paid the first month's rent in advance and bond, if a tenant then defaults on payments, you would have to take court action to have them removed. In this event, the courts would always rule in the landlords favour, BUT, by that time probably six months would have passed (the end of the tenancy). And even though the courts may have ruled in your favour, this doesn't mean that the tenants will pack their bags and leave. If they decide to stick it out, you would then have to apply to the courts again for the bailiffs to physically remove them. This would take approximately another three months as the tenants again have legal rights ensuring them due notice of this event.

So the end result is that you could be left with as much as eight months unpaid rent plus the damages that they would no doubt do and you couldn't begin re-marketing the property until all this process had finished and the property was back in order. You think this doesn't happen? - I've been lucky this has only happened to me twice and I've always been a good honest landlord! So if you are relying on the rent to pay the mortgage and this happens to you, you would be in trouble. And don't think that this wouldn't happen with the expensive 'executive lets', I would be inclined to suggest that this could be at least *as* likely, which would be a disaster if you were under financed.

And if you get mad and physically throw them out, change the locks or even just harass them, YOU could end up in prison. Such is justice - so maybe the Monopoly board is more real than you think!

If a tenant defaults on a payment, the best way to deal with it is to see them in person to discuss the situation calmly. In many cases, the problem is caused by a change in circumstance such as redundancy etc. In this event, they may not even be aware that the social security will in most cases pay the rent or at least some of it. So you could perhaps help them through this with the appropriate forms etc., and show them that you are a human being and not a monster. I've had many such situations which were resolved quite easily this way. In some cases I've even reduced the rent to help them.

Contracts

It's absolutely essential that you make sure that the correct contracts are signed and witnessed BEFORE the tenants are allowed possession of your property - (one signed copy each for tenant and landlord). Failure to get this right could halve the value of your property or worse.

The normal contracts used by property investors is the Assured Short hold tenancy lasting normally 6 or 12 months (but can vary). You can have these drawn up by a solicitor or they can be bought from W.H. Smiths (Oyez forms).

Two months before the end of the tenancy, you should give written notice to the tenant that the contract is due to end (section 28 notice) and then either they will agree to vacate or another contract can follow if both parties agree.

Alternatively, you can allow an open continuation of the contract, but in this instance, you would have to give the tenants two months notice to vacate, but they would only have to give you one month should they wish to vacate.

Should a tenant vacate before a contract ends, legally you would be entitled to pursue them for the rent payable to the end of the contract, but in practice, even if you managed to find them it's doubtful that you would be successful.

If you use an agent, they will normally make a charge to the tenant for the administration of the contract.

Bonds and Advance Payments

It's normal practice for landlords to insist on at least one month's rent plus a bond (deposit) of at least more than a month's rent to be paid in advance. If the tenant can't come up with this amount, don't deal with them however much they beg you. Once they're in your property, you've got the devil's own job to get them out again should things go wrong.

The bond is kept for any damages (excluding wear and tear) or cleaning which may be necessary at the end of the tenancy or rent shortfalls. It should be made clear to the tenant that the bond should not be used as the last month's rent. You (or your agent) must repay the bond to the tenant (assuming no deductions are to be made) within 28 days of the end of the tenancy.

Professional agents are now required to lodge any bond money in an independent deposit protection scheme and *they* will release the money to the tenant unless you can prove damages. In the event of a dispute the ombudsman will always rule in favour of the tenant unless you can prove them to be at fault. It's therefore essential that you have proof of inventory and condition at the outset of the tenancy (photographs signed by the tenant are not a bad idea). But do remember that fair wear and tear must be expected. See http://www.tpos.co.uk for further information

Occasionally, you may find a tenant offering you perhaps six months' rent in advance. Although this may sound wonderful, I would be inclined to be suspicious as this is usually how the cannabis growers operate. And should you let one of them in, they will never be in when you come to check the property, will probably change the locks and will do an enormous amount of damage to your property, as will the police when they smash your doors in!

I've never personally had to deal with cannabis growers, but I did once let a property to a seemingly perfect couple who were into credit card fraud in a big way. I managed to arrive at the property with a key just before the police smashed the door in. He was then imprisoned leaving me with the problem of evicting his then pregnant and unemployed partner who I ended up paying to leave. They incidentally provided very genuine looking forged bank, and employment references - but they were fraudsters!

Prior to them taking possession this property had been totally refurbished and when I managed to regain possession after months without rent, there was also several hundreds of pounds worth of damage.

Property Checks

It's essential that you or your agent make regular checks to your properties. You can't however just barge in, but do have this right by giving due notice to the tenants.

Items that should be checked are:

- Window sills for condensation;
- Extractors (kitchen and bathroom);
- Under kitchen sink (waste pipe leaks);
- Leaks around toilet cistern;
- Tiles around shower or floors for faulty grouting;
- Sealant around showers and sinks;
- Floor sealant in bathroom;
- Washing machine (inlet/outlet leaks);
- Dripping taps;
- Central Heating boiler water pressure;
- Radiators for bleeding (or leaks);
- General condition (visual);
- External air bricks (for blockages);

- Roof, ridge tiles, guttering, and pointing.

Remember that 'a stitch in time saves nine'. The tenants will only inform you of any problem that affects them directly. A leaking washing machines waste pipe will probably not bother them at all, as they won't see it, but bit by bit it will cause severe damage to your property.

Suggest to tenants that the windows should be left in the 'vent' position whenever possible and point out that a property free of condensation is much cheaper to heat.

Finding Tenants

Finding tenants is not rocket science, in fact if you build a reputation as a good honest landlord with multiple properties, very often the tenants will find you. But never let 'friendship' enter the equation. I would never sell a car to anyone who I know, nor would I rent a property to anyone I know. Ignore this at your peril!

Common ways of finding tenants are:

- Local Newspapers;
- 'To Let' board outside property;
- Free Internet sites such as Gumtree and Viva Street;
- Your own website (for multiple properties);
- Letting Agents.

I have to say that using a good agent for full management in my opinion (and personal experience) is worthwhile, but negotiate costs. I pay 10% for full management which is probably a preferential rate. We'll deal more with agents later.

The National Landlords Association

The National Landlords Association offers a whole host of information and services for the private landlord including:

- Tenant Checks;

- Rent Guarantee Insurance;
- Legal Forms and Letters;
- Inventory Checks;
- Rent Arrears;
- Mortgages;
- Free Tax investigation Insurance;
- Conveyancing;
- Energy Performance Certificates;
- Landlord Insurance;
- Plus more.

If intending to proceed without a good agent I would suggest that joining would be very worthwhile. See: http://www.landlords.org.uk for further information.

Chapter 5

Financing Your Project

Gone are the days when anyone could get a 120% mortgage for as much as they wanted, at least for the time being. But to be honest these sorts of deals were very rare anyway. Even when I bought my first 'Buy to Let' property, the building societies would only lend a maximum of 75% and insisted on a minimum 9% yield. At the time I was regularly achieving a 12 - 15% yield so this was never a problem to me. But having said this, at that time the interest rates were much higher (typically 10%+), therefore anything less than a 9% yield was simply not worthwhile. Today (with low interest rates) although a 5% yield is workable (just), you must remember that the higher the yield, the quicker you will increase your portfolio.

Anyway, right now you will probably need a 20 - 25% deposit and the interest rate will typically be 1% higher than a standard mortgage. But apart from this most of the banks and building societies have dreamt up all sorts of new charges that never used to exist, like arrangement fees and early redemption fees etc. And as these can vary considerably, you would be a fool not to shop around.

Repayment Mortgages

Within the 'repayment' mortgage category comes a whole host of variable possibilities, like fixed interest rates, variable rates and trackers etc.

To confuse matters even more, many lenders calculate their interest rates differently - some monthly, some annually and some on a daily basis and this can make a considerable difference particularly when interest rates start rising again - and they will! Without doubt the best type of repayment mortgage is the 'Australian' type arrangement where interest is calculated on a daily basis and any savings that you might have (or even the unused part of your salary) could temporarily be paid into this account to reduce the interest still further. This type of mortgage could save you literally thousands as shown shortly.

But you must remember that all the banks are primarily concerned with their own interests and will consequently try to sell you what is most profitable to them.

Alternatively, you could employ an independent financial advisor, but of course he/she won't be working for nothing either, so do your sums and watch out for hidden charges - it's a minefield!

Just in case you don't know I will explain how a repayment mortgage works.

Assuming you borrow £100,000 over a 20 year period at 6% interest. In the first few years you will pay very little off the capital (the £100,000), but would pay the interest on what you owe. In the later years, once you have paid more off the capital, there would be less interest to pay, so you will then be paying even more off the capital. Payments are calculated so that the debt is cleared at the end of the agreed period and if interest rates change during this period, then payments will be adjusted up or down to compensate.

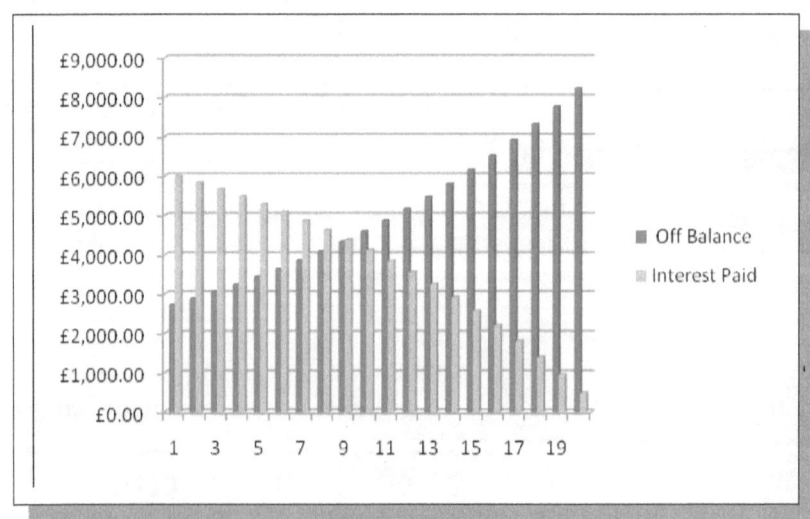

The previous graph shows the differential between interest and capital payments during the course of a twenty year period. Notice that the break point is roundabout year ten.

Should you wish to clear all or part of the mortgage, before the final due date, then a redemption charge will generally be payable and this could be substantial, so make sure that you are fully aware of how much this may be *before* you enter into any arrangement.

Interest Only Mortgages

Interest only mortgages are another possibility and are used quite regularly by investors. In this event, as the name suggests you pay only the interest over an agreed period and then at the end of this period you would still owe the full amount and would have to find the funds to pay for it or sell the property to raise the funds. So in this event you would be assuming that by the time the mortgage ends, the property would be worth substantially more than the amount owed - and you'd almost certainly be correct.

Personally I've never used interest only mortgages, but they are certainly a way of increasing your portfolio quickly, but I would advise caution at least initially. And remember that the interest paid would be far higher as shown shortly.

Life insurance for the term of the mortgage would be required for both repayment and interest only mortgages, but remember that you wouldn't necessarily have to buy this from the lender.

Endowment Mortgages

Endowment and pension mortgages are by and large redundant at the moment although they may re-emerge in improved formats in the future.

Basically these are an interest only mortgage with a 'with profits' endowment life insurance or pension attached. Meaning that theoretically when the endowment policy matures (at the end of the mortgage), this will provide the funds to repay the mortgage in full.

The Real Differences

Careful planning when choosing a mortgage could save you many thousands of pounds. The chart below shows a few variations all at 6%.

£100000 Mortgage at 6%		
	Total Interest	**Payments**
19.5 year Calculated Monthly	£69,767.00	£726.50
20 year Calculated Annually	£74,376.00	£726.50
24.5 year Calculated Monthly	£90,358.00	£652.00
25 year Calculated Annually	£95,527.00	£652.00
20 year Interest Only	£120,000.00	£500.00
25 year Interest Only	£150,000.00	£500.00

Notice the savings that are made if the interest is calculated monthly and the fact that the loan is also paid off earlier for the same monthly payments. Interest calculated on a daily basis produces even more savings particularly if you are allowed to put any savings etc. into the same account even temporarily.

So basically, you choose how much the banks make. But don't forget that these figures assume a constant fixed interest rate of 6%. Over time a fluctuation up and down is inevitable, but at the time of writing this, rates are as low as they'll ever be. Nonetheless the above chart can be used as a guideline as the various examples will alter in the same ratio.

Now, just in case you've not been paying attention, look again at the chart and notice the difference in interest between a 24.5 year repayment mortgage calculated monthly and a 25 year interest only mortgage - it's nearly £60,000 - that's £60k wasted that could be in your pocket!

I have to admit that when I worked this out I was shocked and had to re-calculate the figures.

So in a nutshell when looking for a mortgage you should consider:

a) Deposit required;

b) Arrangement fees;

c) Redemption fees;

d) Interest rate percentage and calculation period (daily/monthly/annually);

e) Length of fixed interest period (if applicable);

f) Details of interest rates after fixed period;

g) Any other hidden fees.

In all cases that you will pay typically 1% extra for a 'buy to let' mortgage or loan.

But remember that you don't *have* to spread your mortgage over 20 or 25 years which seems to be the norm. Clearly the shorter the timescale the less interest you will pay, even though the monthly payments (including capital) will be more.

I was 30 years old when I bought my first property. I originally took out a 20 year endowment mortgage. Shortly after it started I changed this to a repayment mortgage but kept the *with profits* endowment running. Eight years later when we decided to move I took the next repayment mortgage over a twelve year period and also took out an additional endowment to end at the same time as the first.

The end result was that (partially due to other investments) I was mortgage free at 45 years old and still had the benefit of the maturing endowments five years later (which were more than enough to pay off the mortgages that I'd already paid).

Funding your First Deposit

Finding the initial 20 - 25% deposit can often be the biggest stumbling block to your new empire - and this is the same for everyone, me included. If you have enough equity in the property that you live in, this will be the easiest route although of course it will mean taking out a second charge on that property.

If you don't have an existing property, then this is a bigger problem and you may have to start with very low cost investments such as a garage or parking space, but as shown previously these *can* produce excellent yields and may pave your way into the business.

Another low cost entry into the business is to buy a property for multiple/shared occupancy, but live in one room yourself. I know that this is not ideal but it could be an easy way into the business. Sure you will still need the deposit, but assuming you have earnings enough to qualify for the mortgage and you put forward a good enough business plan, you may be able to convince your bank to lower the deposit or at least allow you to borrow this amount from another source as the figures really show that this *is very* viable - even if you were made redundant.

In this event the rent from the other rooms could more than pay the mortgage, and you would naturally save the rent that you would have paid yourself (assuming that you were previously renting somewhere). AND the first £4,250 income would be tax free under the 'rent a room scheme'. Also as you would be living in the property, you would have much more control of the situation and perhaps attract friends as tenants creating a good lifestyle - it doesn't have to be like Rigsby's house!

Compared to the multiple occupancy example shown previously, you will of course be 25% down and consequently the yield would be lower, but you would have had to pay the utility bills and council tax on your previous accommodation, and these could therefore be taken out of the equation. And as you would be in the property, you could lower the utility bills by avoiding wastage which otherwise would be inevitable. Basically you would be getting a free house and a bit further down the line when the equity increases, you could buy another property for yourself and/or expand your letting portfolio.

About 25 years ago I had some dealings with an Asian guy and when I went to call on him I discovered that he and his family lived in one room of a large 6 bed house in Sheffield. At first I thought that he was renting the room, but later discovered that he owned the whole house and was letting all the other rooms out.

Very few English men would get away with cramming their whole family into one room for eating sleeping and living etc. But this guy had *vision*. Now he's a multi millionaire and his wife and family are reaping the benefits of a few years of inconvenience! Anyone can do it - but few can be bothered - or are able to convince their partners of the viability!

Another similar example is where shrewd parents buy a house for multiple occupancy for their son's/daughter's to live in while at University and let the other rooms out to their friends, thus ultimately saving their own rent and paving the way for a low cost entry into the property market for their offspring.

If you already have a mortgage on the property that you live in and intend letting part of the property, you **must** obtain the consent of the lender *before* doing so, in which case the lender may refuse consent or more likely will charge you a higher interest rate (typically 1% extra).

Chapter 6

Presentation

Whatever properties you buy, it's doubtful that they will be decorated and equipped ready to let out, even if they're brand new.

Basically they need to be clean, functional, uncluttered, un-personalised and presented to a *reasonable* standard. If you couldn't live in them yourself, don't expect anyone else to. But spending a fortune on luxury fittings like granite work tops etc. would be stupid - it's the middle way!

One thing that you need to be aware of is that the most likely damage to your properties will come from 'water'. That is: water leaking from the bottom of the shower tray or enclosure; or from the bath (through faulty sealing); or the washing machine (a slight drip from the inlet or outlet pipes over a year could be very damaging); or a leaking toilet cistern; and finally by condensation due to the tenants neglect.

One thing that nearly all tenants have in common is that they don't open windows - some don't even open curtains! And if they dry clothes inside the property, or cook or bath/shower with no ventilation, it's just the same as throwing buckets of water at the internal walls!

Once water has leaked into the floors, if you're lucky it will only cause the floor boards to need replacing. At worst it could rot the joists or cause wet or dry rot. I've had to replace four floors and one joist as a result of water damage.

The way to minimise this problem is to make sure that the tenants are informed of these possibilities, check the properties regularly and have humidistat extractors fitted to the bathrooms and kitchens - these are essential, ignore this at your peril! Unfortunately the law requires that all extractors are fitted with an isolator switch, therefore it must be made clear to the tenants that they must never interfere with it (except in an emergency). They will moan saying that it's their electricity that operates them, to which the answer is that the damage caused without them, would be deducted from their bond. Also make sure that your tenants know exactly where the main water stop tap is and that this is not jammed or too tight.

I once had a tenant who suffered a mains water pipe burst in the kitchen and just went to bed leaving it gushing out. The damage was colossal, but fortunately was covered on the buildings insurance.

It's also not a bad idea to fix humidity gauges to the kitchen and bathroom walls, and then the tenants may be very aware of the potential problems.

If possible UPVC double glazing is ideal unless of course you have a period property where this may devalue it. The price variations for basically the same quality is incredible, so shop around - and don't be taken in by 'if you buy one, you get one free!' Fit windows with 'trickle vents' so that the building is not completely sealed up, as fitting new windows can move condensation issues from the windows to the walls. If you remove fireplaces ensure that the disused flues are vented to prevent dampness building up in them.

Central heating or at least modern electric storage heaters is essential. If fitting a new gas boiler, consider a 'combi' as these create instant hot water and the space where the hot water tank was, could often be used to fit a standalone shower cubicle.

A shower is also essential, either in its own enclosure or over the bath. Gas or electric are both fine. Given the choice of a shower or a bath always choose the shower. But in all cases make sure that the sealing and tiling is sound, more so if you have a power shower. Needless to say a new white bathroom suite with low cost tiles, won't cost a fortune, but makes the place look much more presentable. If doing a re-fit, use a waterproof membrane underneath the floor tiles and behind the shower tiles - available from Topps Tiles.

Laminate floors are low cost to fit (and easy if you want to do it yourself) and far, far more durable than carpets. I would be inclined to use these in the main rooms with a rug, carpets in the bedrooms and tiles or vinyl in the kitchens and bathrooms.

Vertical blinds are a low cost way of dressing the windows in a fairly modern and neutral way. Of course curtains can be used instead or additionally.

In many cases in the kitchens I've got away with just putting in new work surfaces and a new sink assuming that the cupboards are reasonably ok. But if you have to, new low cost units are available from Wickes or B&Q etc.

The ovens and hobs must be clean and in good working order and comply with the necessary safety regulations. Make sure that these are thoroughly clean before the tenants move in and point out that that is how they must leave them or they will be professionally cleaned and the cost deducted from the bond.

Fridge/freezers, washing machines and vacuum cleaners are normally supplied with furnished lettings, but make sure that the fridge doors are left open when the properties are empty and the electric turned off, otherwise the inside will go mouldy! Microwaves and possibly electric kettles can also be an asset.

From the insurance point of view it's better to 'build in' wardrobes, then they come under the 'buildings' insurance and not 'contents'. I've often used the 'Stanley' type sliding door robes which are reasonably priced, fairly easy to fit and look good.

With regards to the rest of the furniture either good modern second-hand or budget new items will suffice. Argos and Ikea should have everything that you need. But keep it simple!

When I first started I used to supply a complete inventory of pots and pans and dishes etc. I since discovered that these items are not really necessary, except for holiday lets. But whatever you have, make sure that you make a detailed list of everything which needs to be checked at the beginning and end of every tenancy.

If your properties have gardens and the tenants are expected to look after these (as in most contracts), then you will need to supply them with the tools to do this - a hover lawn mower, fork, spade and rake should suffice.

I've found that burglar alarms are more of a nuisance than a benefit, but security lighting can be beneficial and of course smoke and gas alarms are essential - more of this shortly.

As with the rest of the presentation, internal and external decorations should be clean and simple. White ceilings and magnolia walls may sound incredibly boring, but it works fine. You could be a little bit more inventive if you like, but don't go over the top - you're more likely to put people off - keep as neutral as possible and always save some paint for touching up. If a property has wall paper when you buy it, you'd be advised to get rid of it, or at least paint over it.

Externally, if a property has a garden, make sure that it is tidy when showing round prospective tenants. But anything more than a simple easy to maintain garden should be avoided. Most tenants simply can't be bothered!

Repairs and Renewals

If you happen to be good at DIY then this is one really major advantage. If not, you need to find yourself a reasonably priced builder/odd job man to take care of any running repairs which *will* occur.

Even a simple plumbing job like fixing a faulty ball cock in the toilet cistern or replacing a rubber washer in a tap would at least require a minimum call out charge which won't be cheap, so the more you can manage yourself the better.

But do remember that anything concerning gas or electricity must be carried out be a qualified professional who should supply you with a written receipt to prove that the job has been undertaken correctly.

EPC Energy Performance Certificates

Energy Performance Certificates are obligatory for all rental properties. These are available reasonably inexpensively via online professionals.

Health and Safety

If you provide furniture in the property, you should ensure that is complies with the Furniture and Furnishings (fire) (safety) Regulations.

All gas appliances must also have annual safety certificates as a legal requirement for all rented properties. If you fail to comply with this regulation you could be fined heavily or even imprisoned. If you use an agent they may arrange this for you, but don't rely on them doing so - it's *your* responsibility!

My plumber does an annual boiler service and includes the safety certificate in the price which only works out at £15 more than the certificate alone!

Any electrical equipment (supplied by you) should be 'PAT' tested (portable appliance testing). So consequently the more appliances that you provide, the more grief you are giving yourself.

You should also carry out a basic health and Safety/Fire Risk assessment of the property to ensure that it is safe for the tenants. The National Landlords Association produce a very good log book for such purposes.

As a minimum you should have a:

- Smoke alarm in the property, preferably mains powered with back up cell (not a battery that the tenants can remove);
- Carbon monoxide alarm;
- Fire blanket in the kitchen;
- Dry powder fire extinguisher on the landing.

You should also ensure that any glazed doors are glazed with safety glass or you can cover them with a safety film to prevent them shattering on your tenants (particularly children) if they slam on them or if they walk into them! This is particularly relevant for patio windows in holiday let's where I would also advise attaching central stickers at eye level for adults and another at a lower level for children. It's so easy to walk into them especially when the sun shines on them (a rare occurrence in the UK)!

Chapter 7

Agents

When I first started I didn't use an agent and to be honest I did pretty well and managed to achieve almost a 100% occupancy on all the properties which was excellent. I did however have numerous problems with some tenants, most of which would have been avoided had I used an agent (which I later did).

Agents charge typically 10 - 15% plus VAT and offer various levels of service from simply finding you tenants to full management. Obviously there are variations with prices and some agents are much better than others.

A good guide is to look for an agent who has been in the letting game for a long time and who is not simply an estate agent doing it on the side. If you use a firm who are chartered surveyors and are regulated by the RICS then you are better protected. They are required to have a complaints handling procedure.

In Sheffield, I use Crapper and Haigh who have been top letting agents for many years - and they are good - both for the tenants and landlords, see: http://www.crapperhaigh.co.uk.

I have had nightmare experiences with other agents, so be warned that they are not all good.

For the difference in price, the full management arrangement is well worth it.

A good agent will:

- Advertise your properties in local property guides, via internet, in their premises, and boards in order to find you suitable tenants;
- Show prospective tenants around your properties;
- Check tenants references;

- Arrange suitable contracts;
- Arrange EPC's where necessary;
- Arrange gas certificates;
- Make regular property checks;
- Deal with meter readings/inventory checks;
- Arrange remedial repairs (at your expense);
- Liaise with tenants on all matters;
- Deal with the bonds and make retentions (for you) at the end of the tenancies when/if necessary.

Furthermore and very importantly, using an agent should enable you to secure a higher rental than you perhaps would have on your own (this alone could go a long way to paying their fees).

My experience can assure you that a *good* agent is well worth the expense, more so if you are new to the business.

Chapter 8

Council Tax & Utilities

In most cases all the utility bills are paid for by the tenants (except in shared houses), but there are nevertheless a few things that you need to be aware of as *you* will become responsible for these when the properties become untenanted.

In all cases make sure that you take meter readings at the beginning and end of every tenancy. Your agent will probably do this, but make sure that you get a copy of the readings.

Council Tax

This is generally the responsibility of the tenant (which must be stated in the contract). But in the case of shared houses this will generally be the landlord's responsibility.

In any event as soon as a property becomes empty, you will have to pay this albeit at a reduced rate. However, there are exceptions, for instance if a property is undergoing any building works, you can apply for an exemption. Also if a tenant vacates before the tenancy expires, the debt will still be theirs and not the landlords.

Water Rates

The landlord is responsible for the water rates as soon as a property is empty unless the property is untenanted and unfurnished, in which case you should let them know.

In many cases it can be to everyone's advantage to have a water meter fitted whereby the tenant pays only for what is used. This is generally cheaper for properties inhabited by one or two people, but probably not for families and definitely not for shared houses where you would be liable for all the wastage.

If a meter is fitted, this theoretically should mean a zero bill when the property is empty, but do check that there are no standing charges. And also remember that if you have a meter and get a burst pipe, in this event you will be liable for the cost of the water wastage, therefore turning the supply off when the property is empty and fixing dripping taps is essential.

Gas & Electricity

Again the tenant would be responsible, and also they would have the right to choose suppliers. But as soon as they move out, the supplier would automatically revert the tariff to their standard rate which is usually 30 - 40% higher than their cheapest 'on line' rate which the tenant probably arranged, Also be warned that even if a property is empty and the utilities turned off, some suppliers charge a daily rate which you could be liable for, even if there are pre payment meters.

If a property is empty during the winter months, it's often worth keeping the heating on low, to keep the place in good order, or if you choose not to do this, you should at least drain the radiators and boiler to avoid burst pipes. And if the electricity is turned off, don't forget to leave fridge doors open otherwise they will go mouldy - I know I said this earlier but it will really pee you off if you forget!

Sometimes in the case of DSS tenants etc., a prepayment meter may have been fitted. These are usually a much higher tariff and you would be wise to have it removed as soon as the tenant vacates.

Some typical rental properties have no gas supply and use either under floor electric heating or electric storage heaters. The advantage of this arrangement is that you will not have to bother with the annual gas safety certificates. Also in this event, it may be cheaper to have an economy 7 or 10 electric tariff. They are not however as flexible as gas central heating and could often result in the tenants not heating the property well which then results in condensation and mould issues.

Telephone/Internet

Once upon a time, when a phone line had been installed in a property, it was just a case of a simple phone call to change users. However, in our present age of 'bureaucracy gone bonkers' this is no longer the case. I'm told that due to the *'data protection act'*, the suppliers will only deal with the account holder - even if he/she happens to have just died! In a recent experience of my own move, I had no alternative but to pay for the installation of another line. I'm not saying that this happens in every case, but be prepared for it.

This problem is beyond your control, but nevertheless very irritating and is more of a problem for the tenants than you. My recommendation would be for them to use a mobile phone and mobile wifi internet such as '3' which I personally use all the time anyway and it works well.

In the case of a shared house, I would recommend not having a land line, as it would be far more trouble than it's worth.

T.V. Licence

This would be the tenant's responsibility and would not be a problem when the property becomes vacant. In the case of a shared house, this would need to be discussed.

Sky T.V.

I have never supplied a satellite dish, but have never objected to tenants installing their own at their expense as long as they agree to make good any damages to decorations etc. However, in the case of flats, planning permission may be required and consent from the freeholder. There may also be objections from other owners so be aware of this. Consequently if the tenant fits one without consent this could cause you problems.

Insurance

You would be wise to have your properties insured for 'buildings' and 'public liability' cover and indeed the former would be a condition of any mortgage or loan.

If you decide to also have 'contents' cover, this would only cover *your* furnishings. It must therefore be made clear to the tenants that if they want cover for their effects, *they* must take out their own cover. 'More Than' offer a reasonable policy for contents only.

I personally never have contents cover, but make sure that as much is built in as possible then this is covered by the 'buildings' policy. For instance, carpets would come under 'contents' cover, whereas a laminate floor and built in wardrobes would be 'buildings' cover. The same goes for a built in cooker and hob as against a standalone cooker.

Some insurance companies (or building societies) will not cover you for properties tenanted by DSS claimants. However, if the tenant becomes unemployed during the tenancy, as has happened to me numerous times, you cannot evict them, but must make the bank and insurance company aware of the situation straight away. They will have no choice but to accept the situation as they will be aware that you cannot evict them.

Community Fees & Ground Rents

Most purpose built flats will be leasehold with probably a low annual ground rent payable and also an annual communal fee or 'service charge' which is likely to be much higher. Some complexes also have a communal buildings insurance which you would be obliged to pay your share of.

A well managed block of flats may have a 'sinking fund' towards future major repairs such as communal redecorating, re-roofing and drive repairs etc. Whilst this usually means the service charge is higher it also follows that the property is more likely to maintain a higher value.

All of these charges are generally the responsibility of the landlord and these should be considered when calculating the yield.

Chapter 9

Tax

You are advised to seek professional guidance from a qualified accountant regarding all accounts and tax issues. The information given here should be taken as a rough guide only.

As a landlord you may be liable for two types of taxes:

- Income tax; and
- Capital gains tax.

Understanding these is the key to avoiding or at least reducing them.

Rental property is not subject to VAT, but your agent's fees will be.

Income Tax

As soon as you begin trading as a landlord you'd be wise to inform the Inland Revenue of your new venture, and after your first year of trading you will need the 'Land & Property' additional sheet to your self assessment tax return form.

As a landlord there are two different types of expenses which you should be aware of:

- Revenue expenses; and
- Capital expenses.

Revenue expenses are claimed via the 'Land & Property' form whereas the Capital expenses are mainly claimed via the Capital Gains Tax form when/if you sell one or more of your investments and are liable for this tax.

The following are revenue expenses:

- Painting/decorating & general maintenance;
- General repairs;
- Council tax (where applicable);
- Utilities (where applicable);
- Legal & professional fees;
- Mortgage interest;
- Ground rent & communal fees;
- Gas certificates;
- Removal/delivery charges;
- Advertising;
- Insurance;
- Proportion of petrol/home telephone/internet/postage etc.

In addition to these a capital allowance can be claimed for such items as lawn mowers/vehicles etc.

On normal lettings a wear and tear allowance for furnishings amounting to 10% of the gross rent received can be claimed. But on holiday lettings a capital allowance can be claimed for all the furnishings *or* the 10% allowance as you choose.

Capital Gains Tax

Capital gains tax is only paid if and when you sell an investment and have made a profit after the capital expenses and allowances have been deducted. Tax is then paid at the lower or higher rates (currently 18% & 28%) depending on your other income.

The following are capital expenses:

- Buying expenses (legal fees etc.);
- Selling fees (agents/legal etc.);
- Mortgage redemption charges;

- Building improvements.

Even if you don't sell an investment you should still keep records of these in your annual accounts, in preparation for when you do sell.

Some expenses could possibly fall into either category, for instance is a laminate floor a building improvement or just maintenance? The same goes for built in wardrobes and many other items. In this event you can only claim it as a revenue expense *or* a capital expense, but not both. As already shown, in the early years, you will almost certainly not make a profit anyway, so where ever you can, it's probably best to claim such items as capital expenses, even though it may be 10 years or more down the line when you actually claim them.

An important point about capital gains tax is that if you buy a property in joint names with your wife or partner (or anyone else) you will both be entitled to the full capital gains allowance (currently £10,600). This can be very important as there is now no taper relief or indexation as there used to be.

Another point to consider is that if you buy say, two low cost properties as against one expensive one, when the time comes to sell, they could be sold in different tax years, thereby doubling the allowances and reducing the liabilities.

The two charts shown here assume that both partners earn £20,000 each which means that any gain per tax year will (at current rates) be taxed at 18% for the first £14,370 (£34,370 less £20,000) and anything above this will be taxed at 28%. You will see that in this event in the first chart, capital gains tax will only be payable at the lower rate, whereas in the second chart, it will be payable partially at the higher rate. Therefore, if making the gain as in the first chart **twice** which would be the same gain as in the second chart, but sold in different tax years (which could even be only one day apart if selling on April 5th and 6th) then a tax saving of £7,954 (£16,306 - £8,352) would result. Not a bad saving for a bit of forward planning!

Couple this with the savings made on a good repayment mortgage with interest calculated daily or monthly, and then far more of the profits will end up in *your* pocket where they should be.

For this reason I've only ever bought fairly low cost properties in joint names with my wife. As a result I have paid very little income tax and minimised the capital gains tax.

Purchase Price	£50,000.00		
Selling Price	£100,000.00		
Capital Gain	£50,000.00		
Buying Fees	£400.00		
Selling Fees	£1,800.00		
Redemption Fees	£400.00		
Building Improvements	£3,000.00		
Total Expenses	£5,600.00		
Joint Allowances	£21,200.00	£10,600.00	each
Total	£26,800.00		
Taxable Gain	£23,200.00	£11,600.00	each
Taxed @ 18%	£23,200.00	£11,600.00	each
Tax Payable	**£4,176.00**	**£2,088.00**	each

Should your and/or your partners normal earnings put either of you in the higher tax brackets, it might be worth hanging onto your investments until you retire and then only pay tax at the lower rates as your income will be less and your tax allowances higher. But capital gains tax rules change all the time so you need to keep your eye on when is the most profitable time for you to sell.

To be honest, with regards to property the rules are most unfair at the moment due to there being no indexation or taper relief, but this could be only temporary. In extreme cases it may be worth your while living abroad for a few years and selling when you are 'non domicile' in the UK and avoid it all, but then you may be liable to pay capital gains tax in your new country of residence. No doubt your accountant will advise of the most tax efficient way.

Purchase Price	£100,000.00		
Selling Price	£200,000.00		
Capital Gain	£100,000.00		
Buying Fees	£500.00		
Selling Fees	£3,000.00		
Redemption Fees	£800.00		
Building Improvements	£6,000.00		
Total Expenses	£10,300.00		
Joint Allowances	£21,200.00	£10,600.00	each
Total	£31,500.00		
Taxable Gain	£68,500.00	£34,250.00	each
Taxable @ 18%	£28,740.00	£14,370.00	each
Tax @ 18%	£5,173.20	£2,586.60	each
Taxable @ 28%	£39,760.00	£19,880.00	each
Tax @ 28%	£11,132.80	£5,566.40	each
Tax Payable	**£16,306.00**	**£8,153.00**	each

DISCLAIMER

Every effort has been made to ensure that the information herein is correct, but as laws and regulations are constantly changing, no responsibility can be accepted for any inaccuracies.

You are therefore advised to seek independent and professional advice before acting on any of the advice contained herein.

Other Books/Guides by Martin Woodward

Your Own Home Run Sign Business
Driving Instructor Training - Exposed!
Use Your Mind to Learn How to Drive
Clutch Control and Gears Explained
The New Driver's Handbook
A Guide to Profitable Self Employment
Magnetic Business Cards for Profit
An Introduction to Traded Options
Keyboard Improvisation One Note at a Time ♪
Learn How to Play Electronic Keyboard or Piano in a Week! ♪
New Easy Original Piano / Keyboard Music - Beginners - Intermediate ♪
Learn to Play Piano / Keyboard With Filo & Pastry - A Beginners Book For Children & Very Silly Adults! ♪
Buying Property and Living in Cyprus

See: www.martinwoodward.net for details of the above

-----oooooOOOOOooooo-----

See: www.deep-relaxation.co.uk for details of items below

Binaural Beat Maker Plus
The Golden Sphere
Relaxation CD's & mp3 Recordings ♪

www.ingramcontent.com/pod-product-compliance
Lightning Source LLC
Chambersburg PA
CBHW021023180526
45163CB00005B/2082